Food and Cooking in
Viking
Times

Written by **Clive Gifford**

Illustrations by **Paul Cherrill**

PowerKiDS
press.
New York

Published in 2010 by The Rosen Publishing Group Inc.
29 East 21st Street, New York, NY 10010

First Edition

Series Editor: Victoria Brooker
Editor: Susie Brooks
Designer: Jason Billin
Picture researcher: Shelley Noronha
Food consultant: Stella Sargeson

Library of Congress Cataloging-in-Publication Data

Gifford, Clive.
  Food and cooking in Viking times / Clive Gifford.
      p. cm. -- (Cooking in world cultures)
  Includes index.
  ISBN 978-1-61532-354-8 (library binding)
  ISBN 978-1-61532-365-4 (paperback)
  ISBN 978-1-61532-366-1 (6-pack)
  1. Cookery, European--History--Juvenile literature. 2. Cookery,
Viking--Juvenile literature. 3. Vikings--Food--Juvenile literature.
  I. Title.
  TX723.5.A1G54 2010
  641.089'395--dc22

                          2009024071

Photographs:
cover and 6 akg-images/Gilles Mermet; 4 Peter Bull; 5, 7, 10, 14,
17 akg-images/Erich Lessing; 8 Werner Forman Archive; 9 Musee
des Antiquites Nationales, St. Germain-en-Laye, France/Lauros/
Giraudon/The Bridgeman Art Library;12, 28 akg-images/Bildarchiv
Steffens; 16 Musee des Antiquites Nationales, St. Germain-en-Laye,
France/Lauros/Giraudon/The Bridgeman Art Library; 18 Museo
della Civilta Romana, Rome, Italy/Roger-Viollet, Paris/The
Bridgeman Art Library; 20 © Layne Kennedy/CORBIS; 21 The
Art Archive/Gianni Dagli Orti; 22: The Art Archive/Gianni Dagli
Orti; 24 The Art Archive/Bardo Museum Tunis/Gianni Dagli Orti;
26 The Art Archive/Museo Prenestino Palestrina/Alfredo Dagli
Orti/Gianni Dagli Orti; 27 The Art Archive/Bardo Museum
Tunis/Gianni Dagli Orti; 29 © Werner Forman/CORBIS

Manufactured in China

CPSIA Compliance Information: Batch #WAW0102PK: For Further Information

contact Rosen Publishing, New York, New York at 1-800-237-9932

Contents

The Viking age

The Vikings is the name given to peoples originally from Denmark, Norway, and Sweden, but in a short period of time, they conquered many other lands. The years between 800 and 1050 CE became known as the Viking Age.

Peaceful start

The Vikings' **ancestors** were peaceful farmers. Historians believe that their population eventually grew so big that there was not enough farmland to support them all. So they went after everyone else's!

Early raids

The Vikings were skilled shipbuilders and sailors. They ruled the seas as traders, explorers, and fierce invaders. In the late eighth century, they made their first raids on Britain, targeting coastal towns, churches, and monasteries to capture treasures and slaves. Later, they sailed up European rivers and attacked inland towns. They also traveled east as far as Russia and south to the Mediterranean Sea.

► *This map shows the great distances Viking ships traveled to invade or trade.*

Major invasions

In the ninth century, the Vikings made bigger invasions. They began to settle in the lands they captured, such as Scotland, much of England, Ireland, Iceland, and northern France and Germany. In their fast **longships**, which were well-designed for quick attacks and getaways, the Vikings were formidable enemies. In 911 CE, the French king granted Normandy to the Vikings to put a stop to their raids.

Revealing remains

The Vikings had a major impact on Europe. They built many farms, villages, towns, and trading routes. **Archaeologists** have found remains of Viking settlements that give us clues about how the Vikings lived. From these, we can get a taste of their food and cooking!

▲ *Viking warriors sail in longships on the way to an invasion. They wore helmets made of iron or leather and used spears, swords, and battle-axes to fight.*

Viking longships

Viking longships were used for raids and invasions. These wooden boats were 60 feet (18 meters) long and just 8.5 feet (2.6 meters) wide. The Vikings used rows of oars and square-shaped sails to power them through the water.

Farms and food

Despite their fearsome reputation, most Vikings were peaceful farmers. They lived in small communities, growing all of their own food, such as cereal crops and vegetables, and rearing **livestock**.

Varied lands

The Vikings farmed lands in a wide variety of climates and soil types. Norway and Sweden were freezing and almost **barren** compared to warmer, **fertile** parts of Denmark. Most Vikings who settled in new lands kept their own farming methods but learned to grow new crops that suited local conditions.

Plowing and planting

Many Viking farmers used a very simple form of plow, called an *ard*. This was pulled along by a horse or oxen, to break up the soil for planting. Cereal crops, such as barley, were sown in the spring and harvested in the fall. The stalks of the crop made straw, which was fed to farm animals.

▶ *This Viking wooden wagon called an Oseberg Cart was used for transporting hay from farm fields.*

Fruit and vegetables

In the right climates and soils, the Vikings grew vegetables such as cabbages, leeks, turnips, onions, and beans. Often, there was a vegetable patch near the house, with herbs including dill, mint, and chervil. Many Viking farms had a small orchard for growing fruits such as apples, plums, blackberries, and bilberries. Berries from bushes and trees were also eaten.

Grazing animals

Farm animals in Viking times were much smaller and less plump than those of today. All farms had cows, whose milk was often made into cheese. They also kept pigs, goats, horses, chickens, and geese. During the summer, some animals were taken to graze away from the farm, on land called a *shieling* or pasture. In the fall, farmers would select their weakest animals for slaughter.

▲ *This selection of Viking farm tools includes two early ax heads, a knife with a handle made of animal bone, a bone needle, and shears (like strong scissors) made of iron.*

Meat and more

Almost every part of a slaughtered animal would be used in some way. The meat would be dried, smoked, or salted to **preserve** it. The skin would be **tanned** into leather for clothes and other items. Bones were carved into household tools.

Bread

Bread was an important part of the Vikings' diet. Baking was a daily task because the bread was usually stale by the next day.

Making flour

The Vikings made bread using barley, wheat, rye, or oats, depending on what grew best in their region. The grain had to be harvested and separated from its stalk. Then it was ground into flour. The mill used for grinding was made of two stones, with a handle that turned one stone around. Winding the handle was dull, tiring work, often given to slaves.

▲ *The Vikings ground grain between two large circular stones to make flour. The bottom stone was called a quern and the top stone, a handstone.*

Baking bread

The Vikings baked mostly flat breads and oatcakes without yeast. But sometimes they left some flour and water to **ferment** into a bubbling **sourdough**. This helped bread to rise. There were no ovens, so baking was done on trays raised just above a fire.

Tree bark bread

Some Vikings used the inner layer of bark from the birch tree to make flour! It gave the bread a rich, sweet taste. Nuts, seeds, or herbs could also be used to flavor the dough.

Fruit-topped oatcakes

You can experiment with this simple recipe by adding 2–3 tablespoons of honey or some chopped walnuts to the dough.

Serves 4

You will need:

1¾ cup (225g) whole-wheat flour
1¼ cup (100g) oatmeal
¼ teaspoon salt

½ tablespoon vegetable oil
¾ cup (175ml) water
2–4 apples, peeled and cored
Handful of berries—ideally blackberries, but raspberries or blackcurrants will do

1. Mix together the flour, oatmeal, and salt in a mixing bowl. Combine the oil and water in a jug and slowly add to the flour mixture to make a sticky dough.

2. Knead the dough with the heels of your hands for 1 minute. Shape the dough into a ball and put it back in the bowl.

3. Cover the bowl with a damp cloth and leave in a warm place for 30–40 minutes until the dough is stiff.

4. Cut the apples into chunks, then crush them to a pulp using a pestle and mortar or potato masher. Crush and mix in the berries.

5. Roll small pieces of the risen dough into balls. Flatten these into disks ⅛ in. (3mm) thick, on a lightly floured surface.

6. Heat a griddle or large, lightly oiled frying pan and cook the oatcakes for about 2 minutes per side until they are golden.

Flip them onto a plate and spread the fruit on top.

Life in the longhouse

Viking families lived all together in big groups in a longhouse. This traditional home was usually made of wood or sometimes stone. The roof was thatched or covered in turf.

One room

A longhouse had no dedicated kitchen. The Vikings rarely divided their homes into separate rooms, although they did section off one end as a shelter for valuable livestock. Some houses had small openings in the walls to let in light, but there was no glass for windows. Fresh straw was regularly spread on the dirt floor.

Smoke and fire

In the middle of the longhouse was a large cooking fire. Sometimes a chimneylike hole was made in the roof above it, but the room would still get smoky. Viking families often hung meats and fish high in the longhouse, where the smoke would help to preserve them.

Cooking area

The area around the fire was cluttered with barrels, chests, and sacks full of flour, grain, and vegetables. Clay jars held herbs, oils, milk, nuts, and honey. The Vikings usually prepared food on a floor mat, or on a platform by the wall that doubled as a bed. Women did all of the cooking, sometimes helped by young children.

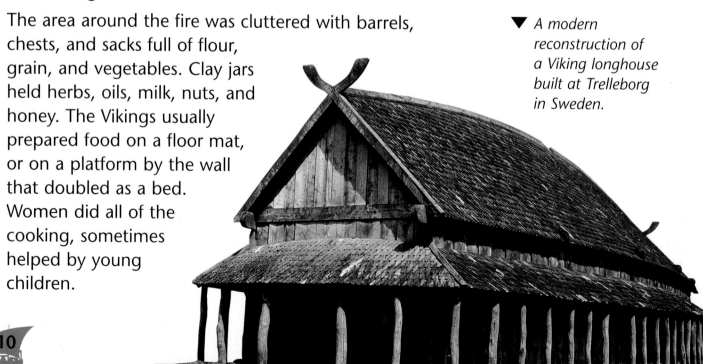

▼ A modern reconstruction of a Viking longhouse built at Trelleborg in Sweden.

Honey-glazed root vegetables

The Vikings had no sugar, but they loved honey. They even used it to sweeten some savory dishes, like these mouth-watering roasted vegetables.

Serves 4

You will need:

3 carrots
1 turnip
¼ white cabbage
1 large leek

2 tablespoons (30g) butter, cut into small pieces
Salt and pepper
2 tablespoons honey

1. Peel the carrots and turnip. Chop these and the other vegetables into medium-sized chunks.

2. Heat the oven to 400°F (200°C). Meanwhile, boil the turnip and carrots in a pan of water for 3 minutes, then drain.

3. Place all the vegetables in an ovenproof dish. Scatter the butter, salt, and pepper over the top. Cover the dish with foil.

4. Cook for 20 minutes in the oven. Then remove the dish, take off the foil, stir, and drizzle the honey on top. Cook another 20–30 minutes without the foil and serve.

The meal-fire

At the center of most Viking homes was a large fire on which all meals were cooked. This was called the *máleldr*, meaning "meal-fire."

Cooking kettle

The Vikings cooked most of their food by boiling. They would do this in a kettle—a large cauldron or pot made of iron or **soapstone**. This was sometimes hung on a chain from the ceiling and lowered into the fire for cooking. Stews and soups were cooked in the kettle, often using the remains of the previous night's dinner.

▲ *Viking women were in charge of preparing all the ingredients used to make a meal.*

Roasting and baking

Long skewers made of iron were used as **spits** to roast joints of meat or whole fish. The Vikings also liked to wrap meat or fish in leaves and bury them in the ground under the fire to cook slowly. Some cooks kept a pit beside the fireplace, which they filled with hot ashes and lumps of glowing, burned wood. This was used for baking or frying food on trays or pans.

Cooking stones

To warm up liquids like milk or soup, the Vikings often used cooking stones. These were ordinary rocks, heated in the fire and then placed in the kettle or pot. Once the stones had given up their heat, they were taken out.

Chicken and herb soup

The Vikings made many soups in their kettles. This recipe uses chicken stock instead of Viking ale, and a large pan in place of the kettle.

Serves 4-6

You will need:

12 oz. (350g) chicken pieces
2 carrots
1 onion
1¾ tablespoons (25g) butter

2 pints (1 liter) hot chicken stock
2–3 handfuls of fresh herbs, such as cress, marjoram, dill, or thyme. If you can find them, add dandelion leaves just as the Vikings would.
⅜ cup (100ml) cream

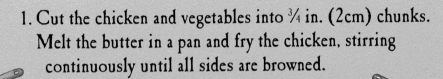

1. Cut the chicken and vegetables into ¾ in. (2cm) chunks. Melt the butter in a pan and fry the chicken, stirring continuously until all sides are browned.

2. Pour all the chicken and juices into a large pan, add the vegetables and stock, and bring to boil.

3. Wash and chop the herbs and leaves and add to the pan.

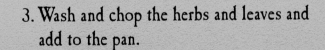

4. Turn down the heat and simmer for 30–40 minutes. Check that the chicken is tender and cooked through.

5. Stir in the cream and simmer for another few minutes before serving.

Mealtimes

The Vikings ate two meals a day. They would begin their working day and then eat their first meal after around two hours of work.

Day meal

Dagverðr, meaning "day meal," was served in the morning. It usually involved a filling porridge, sometimes sprinkled with chopped nuts or fruit. The remains of last night's dinner might also be reheated and served. Young children were given bread dipped in milk.

Night meal

The main meal of the day was *náttverðr*, or night meal. This was eaten right after work. Darkness fell earlier in the winter than in the summer, so the time of this meal varied. *Náttverðr* was a sociable time, based around the meal-fire for light and warmth.

▼ *The inside of a reconstructed Viking home. A low bench with a mat and a fur blanket are on the left next to the woodpile used to fuel the fire.*

Serving food

Viking homes had very little furniture, so families ate their meals on the floor or at a low wooden table or chest. Most food was served in wooden bowls or on long plates known as trenchers. The Vikings ate with their fingers and spoons, using their iron hunting knives to cut and spear pieces of food. The only type of fork they used was a large one for fishing pieces of meat out of the pan.

▲ *These remains are of Viking bowls and spoons shaped from wood.*

Lively times

During *náttverðr*, people would talk and tell stories, including exciting adventure tales known as **sagas**. Many legends and beliefs were passed down through families in this way, because few Vikings knew how to write. Wooden board games, music, and physical sports such as wrestling were popular after-dinner activities.

Viking craftmanship

The Vikings were excellent craftspeople. They made many beautiful spoons out of wood, bone, or animal horn, carving them with designs such as rope knots or the heads of **mythical** creatures.

Towns and trade

Although most Vikings lived in the countryside, they also built large villages and towns for trading. Town life was quite different for people used to being on a farm.

► *A painting of a typical Viking port scene. It shows a tent on the deck of a ship used to provide cover and storage space. Townspeople look on as the ship is loaded with supplies.*

Trading places

The Vikings traded mainly by ship, so they built their towns on the coast or near rivers that led to the sea. Birka in Sweden and Hedeby in Denmark were the largest known towns in the Vikings' homelands. Other major settlements included Kaupang in Norway, Dublin in Ireland, and Stamford, Lincoln, and York in England.

Busy lives

Life in a Viking town was cramped, bustling, noisy, and smelly. Houses were built very close together, though they still had some space for a storeroom or workshop.

Many town dwellers were traders or craftspeople, selling or making anything from cups and cookware to jewelry. Others worked on fields and farms outside the town.

Garden plots

Most townhouses had an open yard area, where herbs and fruit trees might be grown. Larger households could fit in a patch for vegetables such as peas, beans, and celery. Some people even kept livestock, though there was usually only space for a few pigs or goats. Chickens and geese were allowed to roam the streets, feeding on piles of rubbish.

▼ *Three Viking coins, believed to have been made in Denmark. The first two show designs of merchant ships.*

Markets

Viking towns rarely had places to eat out. People cooked almost all their food at home, using similar methods to those on the farm. They bought and sold ingredients, crafts, and cookware in busy town markets. Here, traders also sold food and spices from other lands.

Jorvik

In 866 CE, the Vikings invaded the Roman town of York. They named it Jorvik, and it grew to be a major trading center and the Viking capital of northern England. By the year 1000 CE, an estimated 10,000 people lived in Jorvik. Archaeological digs in the city have taught us a lot about Viking town life.

Food from the water

Living close to water had advantages other than trade. The Vikings got much of their food from rivers, lakes, and the sea.

Fresh fish

Sea fish, especially cod and herring, were regularly on the menu in Viking coastal towns. Some fishermen speared fish or caught them with a hook and line off a boat. Others may have used nets. Haddock, ling, coalfish, mackerel, and smelt were all common catches.

In lakes and rivers, the Vikings fished for salmon, trout, eels and some freshwater shellfish, such as oysters. Archaeologists have found evidence that the Vikings in Britain ate freshwater fish including pike, perch, roach, and bream.

Fish forever

In the dry, cold north of Sweden and Norway, fish was easily dried and preserved. Local Vikings produced rock-hard *skreið*, meaning "sharp-fish," which they ate like a cracker with butter or cheese. Elsewhere, fish could be preserved in barrels of salt. Salted fish was often transported and traded with people inland.

Whale hunting

Some Vikings along the coasts of Scandinavia and Iceland hunted whales. Mostly, they used boats to drive the whales ashore and then they attacked them with poisoned arrows. The meat, bones, and fatty **blubber** were all put to good use.

▶ *This rock shows a picture of a whale. The lines may have shown how it was to be divided up among the people of a village.*

Fish steaks in herb butter

The Vikings sometimes flavored butter with herbs, which you can use here to make a tasty, yet simple, dish.

Serves 4

You will need:

1 tablespoon fresh parsley
1 tablespoon fresh dill
7 tablespoons (100g) soft butter

Black pepper
4 cod or haddock fillets

1. Chop the parsley and dill as finely as possible.

2. Mash the butter in a bowl and mix in the herbs and pepper thoroughly.

3. Place the butter on a sheet of plastic wrap and roll into a log. Put this in the refrigerator for 20 minutes.

4. Lay the fish fillets skin-side down on a broiler rack. Place a slice of the herb butter on top of each. Put the rack in the broiler pan with an ovenproof dish underneath.

5. Grill for about 10–15 minutes (check the instructions on the fish pack). When the fish is firm and cooked through, pour butter that has dripped into the dish on top. Serve with french fries or honey-glazed root vegetables (see page 11).

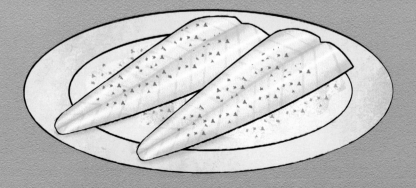

Hunting and gathering

The Vikings added to their diet by hunting wild animals and birds, especially in wintertime. Gathering wild plants also helped people to survive when good farmland was scarce.

Wild meats

A Viking hunter would kill and eat almost any wild animal he came across. In northern lands, this might include moose, reindeer, hare, **elk**, and near the coast, seals. Bows and arrows or spears were the main hunting weapons. Simple traps were also used to **snare** and capture smaller animals, including rabbits, otters, and squirrels.

Family tasks

Children might help their family by gathering wild birds' eggs, fruits, and herbs. Men were in charge of hunting, but women would prepare the meat. This meant cutting up the carcasses and preserving the joints—a tough job, which often took all night. Sometimes it was done in a separate building called a *soðhús*, or cooking house.

▼ *A Viking man wears an animal skin over his shoulder. He is armed with a spear made of iron and wood.*

Hunting helpers

Many Vikings trained dogs and birds of prey, such as hawks and falcons, to help with their hunting. The birds could kill hares, squirrels, and other wild birds, from pigeons to seagulls. The dogs would help to corner an animal or retrieve it.

Pork stew

Wild pigs would be cooked in a large stew in the kettle over the fire. This recipe replaces wild animals with pork and a selection of vegetables.

Serves 4-6

You will need:

1 lb. 2 oz. (500g) lean pork without bones
6 cups (1.4 liters) of water
3 marrowbone pieces that will fit in your pan
3 carrots, peeled
2 leeks

2 celery sticks
1 medium onion
2 cooking apples
1 tablespoon mixed herbs
⅔ cup (50g) oatmeal
Salt and black pepper

1. Chop pork into 1½ in. (4cm) cubes and place in a large pan with 6 cups (1.4 liters) of water. Add the marrowbones.

2. Bring the water to boil. As it boils, use a small sieve to skim the fat off the top. Then cover with a lid, turn down the heat, and leave to simmer for 2 hours.

3. Chop the carrots, leeks, celery, and onion into small pieces. Peel and core the cooking apples and chop into chunks.

4. Remove the marrowbones from the stew and add the carrots, leeks, celery, onion, and herbs. Cook for a further 15 minutes.

5. Add the chopped apple and the oatmeal and stir in thoroughly. Bring the stew to boiling point and cook for 10 more minutes.

6. Season with salt and pepper and serve the stew with chunks of warmed, fresh bread.

Trading trips

The Vikings were renowned sailors using their well-crafted ships to travel long distances. This allowed them to trade with peoples as far away as North Africa and the Middle East, as well as settling in Britain, Ireland, Iceland, and Greenland.

Good swaps

Dried and salted fish were probably the only foods that the Vikings took to trade. Mostly, they sold goods such as animal furs, woollen cloth, soapstone, and amber beads and jewelry. Sometimes they might trade a slave who had been captured in a raid. In return, they received food, glassware, silk, gold, wine, and exotic spices, especially from the Middle East and from Chinese and Persian traders in Russia.

Storage ships

The Vikings used their narrow, fast-moving longships mainly for raids and invasions. They built wider-bodied ships, called knarrs or knorrs, to carry their trading loads. Livestock and other goods were stored in an open area, or well, in the middle of the boat.

▼ *This is a replica of a ninth century Viking ship found in Norway. It is made from oak and pine wood.*

Food on board

Life on a long-distance trading ship was harsh, and sailors had limited food rations. Smoked and salted meats, fish, cheese, and butter would be packed tight in wooden barrels. Some ships carried live goats or cows for milk, or chickens to provide eggs. Wooden tubs of nuts, fruit, and vegetables were also stored aboard.

▲ A Viking trading ship leaving Norway. It is laden with supplies to feed the crew as well as goods to trade with other peoples.

Stopping ashore

The Vikings had no maps or compasses, but they were skilled **navigators**. They used the position of the sun and stars, the winds, and the flights of seabirds as guides. By following coastlines, they could stop ashore at night. This allowed them to add to their food stocks, either by raiding settlements or by gathering wild plants and hunting animals.

Vikings in America

The Vikings settled in Iceland in the tenth century CE. In around 982 CE, they began to reach Greenland. Viking stories tell of Leif Ericsson sailing even farther west, to land in North America in the early eleventh century. Archaeologists have found remains of Viking-like buildings at L'Anse aux Meadows in Newfoundland, Canada.

Viking drinks

Water supplies in Viking towns were often contaminated with sewage and were far from safe. So most Vikings drank other things—particularly a type of beer called ale.

Ale for all

Even Viking children drank ale. It was alcoholic, but relatively weak, and was cloudy and often very sweet. The main ingredient was barley, but a variety of herbs and even fruits could be added. Water was used, too, though it was boiled first to kill any germs.

From water to wine

Clean water was easier to find in streams in the countryside. There was also milk from cows and goats, which could be turned into watery **buttermilk**. Some Vikings made cider from apples and pears. Others used honey to produce a sweet, winelike drink called **mead**. Only the wealthy could afford regular wine. This was usually traded from grape growers in Italy, France, and parts of Germany.

▲ *A female Viking might have used these items: a **drinking horn**, a decorative iron feasting knife, and a pair of iron shears.*

Drinking vessels

The Vikings drank out of flasks, goblets, and cups made of metals, wood, and animal horn. Glasses were rare and valuable. In the Old Norse language, goblets and other drinks holders made of glass were known as *hrimkaldar*, meaning "frost-cups."

Fruit and honey punch

This is one of the few drinks that Vikings made that did not contain alcohol!

Serves 4

Ingredients

2 or 3 apples
If possible, some apple tree leaves

A large handful of blackberries
4¼ cups (1 liter) water
⅜ cup (100ml) honey

1. Remove the cores from the apples but leave the peel on and chop them as finely as possible.

2. Put the apple in a pan with the leaves and blackberries and pour the water in. Bring to boiling point.

3. Let the mixture bubble gently for about 10 minutes, then add the honey.

4. Take the pan off the heat and let it cool for a few minutes. Serve the punch warm in mugs.

Viking feasts

Feasts provided a welcome relief from the harshness of everyday life, and Vikings threw themselves into feasts with great enthusiasm. Feasts in the winter might extend into many days of eating, drinking, and dancing.

Party seasons

In their homelands, the Vikings had three major feasts per year. *Sigrblot* was held in late spring, *Vertablot* in late summer or early fall, and *Jolablot* in midwinter. The word *blot* means sacrifice, or offering, and a horse was sacrificed at the start of each feast. It would then be roasted over an open fire on a giant spit. Other animals, including deer, pigs, and cattle, might be roasted, too, or cut up and cooked in large, bubbling stews. Vegetables and breads were served on the side.

Making merry

In many Viking towns, an event such as the birth of a son or a wedding would be celebrated with a feast. Most people washed down their food with ale drunk from hollowed-out cow horns or deer antlers, known as drinking horns. These were passed around the tables and refilled by the women of the family.

▲ *A selection of typical foods served at a Viking feast. These include preserved meats, tubs of fruit and vegetables, and grains served on long trencher plates.*

More than enough

The richest Vikings held lavish feasts, with plenty to eat and drink for days. Guests brought gifts for their hosts, and hung up their weapons to show that they came in peace. Wine might be served on these occasions, along with gallons of mead and ale. We believe that feasts ended when people were too drunk to eat, drink, or talk anymore, or had already fallen asleep at the table.

Great entertainment

Entertainment at a major feast might include singing, dancing, acrobats, and jugglers. Wealthy hosts often brought in traveling poets, known as *skalds*. A *skald* would be paid to recite poems, and sometimes sagas, from memory. To gain favor with the host of the feast, they made up a poem, called a *drapa*, that praised the host. If it went down well, the poet might receive a gift of jewelry.

▲ *Large Viking jugs were made from clay.*

Wrestling riots

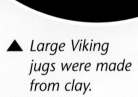

The Vikings loved to wrestle at feasts. Occasionally, an after-dinner wrestling contest would break out into real fighting. Part of the problem was the large amount of alcohol drunk, especially by the men.

Off to Valhalla

The Vikings worshiped a large number of gods who they believed influenced their daily lives and lived in a mythical place called Asgard. Chief of all their gods was Odin, who lived in a hall called Valhalla. Many Vikings later converted to Christianity.

Popular gods

Different gods influenced different areas of the Vikings' lives. Among the most important was Thor, son of Odin, who loved feasts and fighting and was in charge of law and order. For farmers, Freyr, the god of fertility and the environment, was their most important god. He was responsible for good weather and healthy crops. Freyr's twin was Freya, the goddess of love and death.

Worship and charms

The Vikings probably worshiped both at home and in the open air. They certainly made sacrifices of animals, food, and even people, to their gods. They also kept religious charms. Many people wore charms shaped like Thor's hammer, called *Mjollner*, to keep evil spirits away.

▶ *A Viking tapestry of three of their gods (from left to right): Odin holding an axe, Thor carrying his hammer, and the goddess, Freya.*

A whole new world

The Vikings believed in life after death. They usually buried their dead with various belongings, to help them in the next world. A poor person might be buried in his or her best clothes, with a few possessions and some food. Wealthy Viking leaders were often placed in a ship, along with many riches and sometimes horses and slaves, who were killed for the purpose. The ship was then set alight and later, the ashes buried.

The best way to die

For most Vikings, the very best way to die was in battle. This meant that their final journey would be made in the company of the gods to Valhalla, where they would live a life of constant feasting and fighting. They also believed that peasants and those who lived a good life were gathered up by Thor and taken to his great hall in Asgard, called *Bilskirnir*.

▲ *The Viking burial site of Lindholm Hoje in Denmark. Stones mark the sites of hundreds of graves, some in boatlike patterns.*

Bloodthirsty ceremony

At Lejre in Denmark and in Uppsala in Sweden, there was a large festival to honor the gods every nine years. At Lejre, this event was said to be bloodthirsty, with 99 men and 99 horses sacrificed and hung from trees.

Glossary

ancestors people from the distant past that a person is related to and descended from.

archaeologists people who study human life in the past by finding and examining ancient items.

barren land that is hard to grow crops or other plant life on.

blubber a thick layer of fatty tissue found under the skin of whales and some sea mammals including seals.

buttermilk sour-tasting liquid left after milk has been turned into butter.

drinking horns an animal horn used as a cup for drinking at feasts and other occasions.

elk a large species of deer.

ferment types of chemical reactions including ways of converting sugar in foods into alcohol.

fertile when used about land, it means that the soil and conditions are good for growing crops.

livestock animals kept on a farm or elsewhere by people to eat, use their milk, eggs, or wool, or to sell or trade at market.

longhouse a type of home built by the Vikings with usually only one room.

longship a type of ship built by the Vikings that was long and narrow so as to move quickly through the water.

mead alcoholic drink made using honey.

mythical something that is imaginary and not found in real life.

navigators people in charge of finding the way on land or at sea.

preserve ways to keep food from spoiling so that it can be eaten at a later date.

sagas stories told during Viking times about the adventures of heroes or families.

snare an animal trap using a loop of string, rope, wire, or vine that fastens around the leg or body of a creature.

soapstone a type of rocky mineral that can be carved and shaped to form statues and bowls.

sourdough a way of making bread using flour and water that is left to ferment before being added to the rest of the ingredients.

spit a long spike on which meat or fish were speared and then roasted over an open fire.

tanned when the skin of an animal such as a cow is preserved to make leather for clothing or other objects.

Further Information and Web Sites

Books

Everyday Life in Viking Times by Hazel Mary Martell (Sea to Sea Publications, 2005)

Life of the Ancient Vikings by Hazel Richardson (Crabtree Publishing, 2005)

People of the Ancient World: The Vikings by Virginia Schomp (Children's Press, 2005)

Web Sites

Due to the changing nature of Internet links, PowerKids Press has developed an online list of Web sites related to the subject of this book. This site is updated regularly. Please use this link to access this list:
http://www.powerkidslinks.com/ciwc/viking/

Index